An Animal Guessing Game

Who Am I?

Steve Jenkins & Robin Page

HOUGHTON MIFFLIN HARCOURT • BOSTON • NEW YORK

I have...

a sticky,
flicky
tongue,

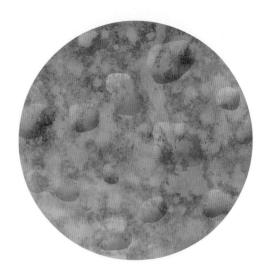

bumpy
green
skin,

two bulging
eyeballs,

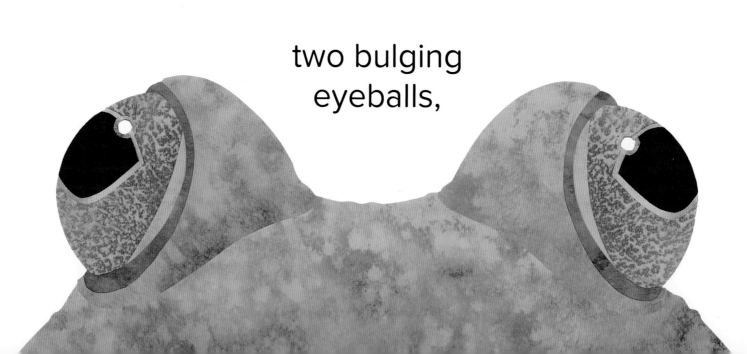

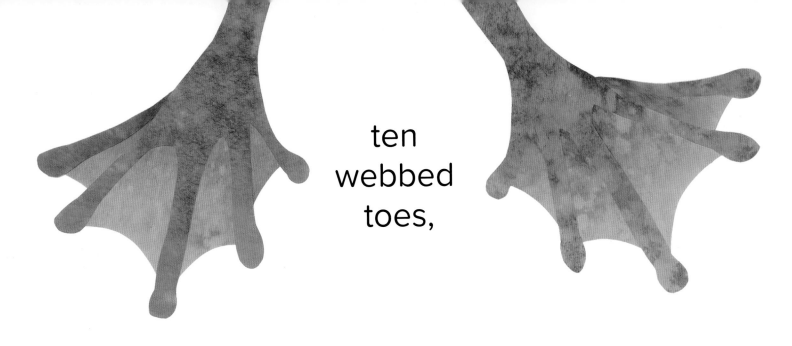

ten
webbed
toes,

a floating lily pad,

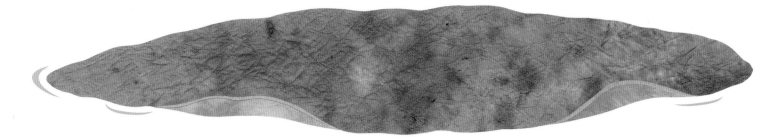

and a fly
for lunch!

Who am I?

I'm a frog!

I have...

springy
back
legs,

a fluffy white tail,

I'm a rabbit!

a twitchy
pink nose,

two long, furry ears,

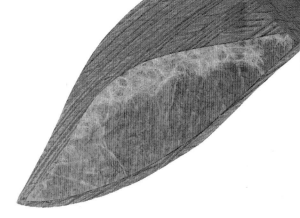

and a carrot
to munch!

Who am I?

I have . . .

a big
pinchy
claw,

two
stalky
eyes,

eight
scuttling
legs,

a tough blue shell,

and a
fish to
catch!

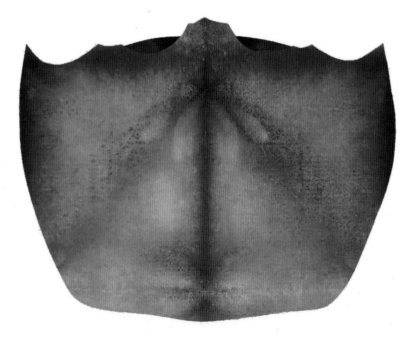

Who am I?

I'm a crab!

I have...

a pink and black beak,

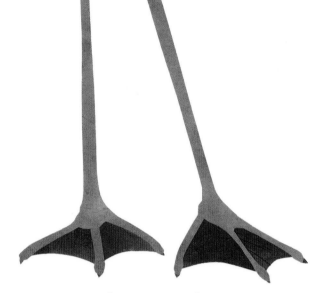

two skinny legs,

bright, colorful feathers,

a long
curvy
neck,

a single white egg,

and a nest
made of mud.

Who am I?

I'm a flamingo!

I have . . .

two round yellow eyes,

soft, silky
feathers,

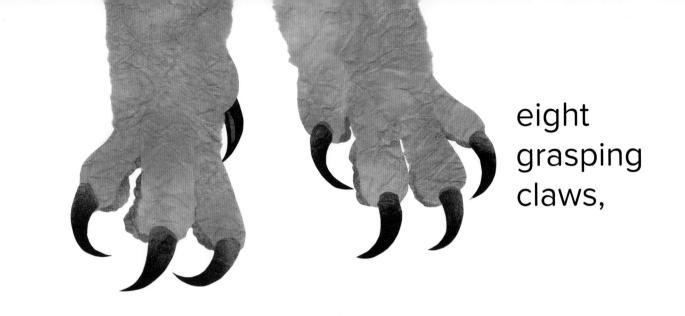

eight
grasping
claws,

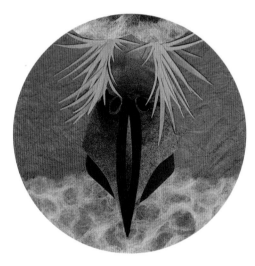

a sharp
black
beak,

and a
mouse for
a snack!

Whoooo am I?

I'm an owl!

I have...

a long
grippy
tail,

ten nimble
toes,

eight
clever
fingers,

soft
brown fur,

and a
banana
to eat!

Who am I?

I'm a monkey!

I have...

two touchy
antennae,

nine
black
spots,

two
delicate
wings,

six
wiggly
legs,

two beady eyes,

and a
flower
for a
home.

Who am I?

I'm a ladybug!

American Bullfrog

What do I eat?
Insects, mice, snakes, fish, birds, and other small creatures.

An interesting fact about me:
My croaking call sounds like the mooing of a cow. That's where the name "bullfrog" comes from.

My **bulging eyeballs** let me look around while the rest of my body stays underwater.

My **webbed feet** make me a good swimmer.

Where do I live?
In freshwater ponds, streams, and marshes in North and South America, Europe, and parts of Asia.

How big am I?

Cottontail Rabbit

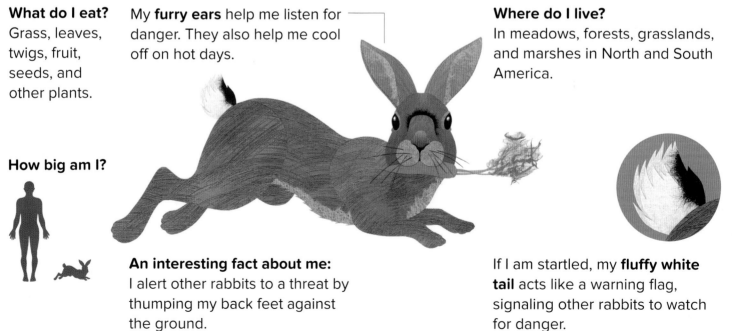

What do I eat?
Grass, leaves, twigs, fruit, seeds, and other plants.

My **furry ears** help me listen for danger. They also help me cool off on hot days.

How big am I?

An interesting fact about me:
I alert other rabbits to a threat by thumping my back feet against the ground.

Where do I live?
In meadows, forests, grasslands, and marshes in North and South America.

If I am startled, my **fluffy white tail** acts like a warning flag, signaling other rabbits to watch for danger.

Ghost Crab

What do I eat?
Clams, snails, baby turtles, lizards, fish, and small crabs.

My **stalky eyes** swivel so I can look in a complete circle.

Where do I live?
On the sandy shores of tropical and subtropical oceans throughout the world.

How big am I?

An interesting fact about me:
I walk and run sideways because of the way my knees bend.

I rub the bumps on my **big pinchy claw** against my shell to make a sound. It helps me communicate with other crabs.

Flamingo

What do I eat?
Shrimp, snails, and algae.

An interesting fact about me:
My pink color comes from the things I eat, including the shells of shrimp.

Where do I live?
In the shallow coastal waters of Central and South America, Africa, and parts of Asia.

How big am I?

I turn my head and **beak** upside down to filter food from the water.

My **skinny legs** are good for wading in the water. I often stand on one leg while I eat. Scientists aren't sure why I do this.

What do I eat?
Other birds, frogs, rodents, and small mammals.

Where do I live?
In deserts, wetlands, forests, grasslands, and cities throughout most of the Americas.

With my **soft, silky feathers** I can fly without making a sound.

How big am I?

An interesting fact about me:
I can hear a mouse creeping along under a foot of snow.

My **round yellow eyes** are large to help me see where I'm going in the dark.

Spider Monkey

What do I eat?
Fruit, nuts, seeds, insects, bird eggs, leaves, and flowers.

An interesting fact about me:
I have four fingers on each hand, but no thumb.

Where do I live?
In the tropical rainforests of Central and South America.

How big am I?

My **grippy tail** has a hairless pad on the underside that helps me hold on to tree branches.

My **ten nimble toes** can grasp branches like fingers on a hand.

Ladybug (Ladybird Beetle)

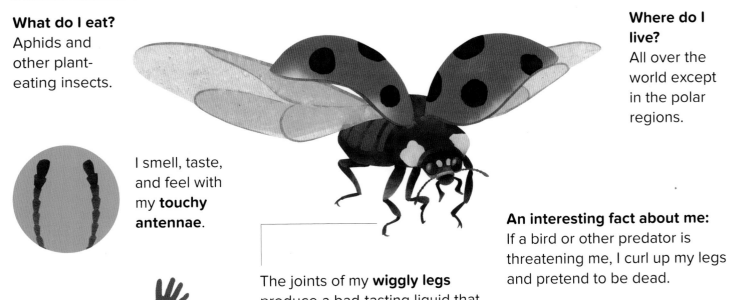

What do I eat?
Aphids and other plant-eating insects.

I smell, taste, and feel with my **touchy antennae**.

How big am I?

The joints of my **wiggly legs** produce a bad-tasting liquid that predators do not like.

Where do I live?
All over the world except in the polar regions.

An interesting fact about me:
If a bird or other predator is threatening me, I curl up my legs and pretend to be dead.

To find out more about these animals

Amazing Animal Facts. By Jacqui Bailey. Dorling Kindersley, 2003.

The Book of North American Owls. By Helen Roney Sattler. Houghton Mifflin, 1998.

Creatures of the Sea—The Crab. By Kris Hirschmann. KidHaven Press, 2003.

Encyclopedia of Animals. Chartwell Books, 2013.

Frogs. By Nic Bishop. Scholastic Nonfiction, 2008.

Frogs and Other Amphibians. By Bobbie Kalman. Crabtree, 2005.

Ladybugs. M.C. McBee. Child's World, 2003.

National Geographic Animal Encyclopedia. By Lucy Spelman. National Geographic Children's Books, 2012.

Usborne World of Animals. By Susanna Davidson and Mike Unwin. Usborne, 2009.

For Ross and Earl —SJ & RP

www.hmhco.com

The illustrations are cut- and torn-paper collage.
The text is set in Proxima Nova Soft and Bernard MT Condensed.

ISBN: 978-0-544-93539-6

Manufactured in China
SCP 10 9 8 7 6 5 4 3 2 1
4500666744

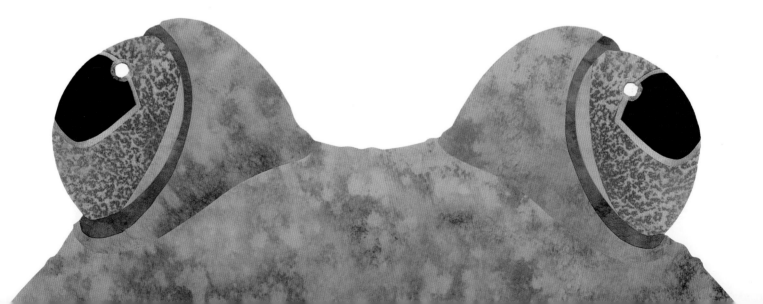